The Four Frogs

AN INCREASINGLY NUMERICAL TALE

✷ INTENSELY TOLD ✷

ABSTRACT:
A Fresh Fable Finds Four Flummoxed **Frogs** Fixing a
Fiendish Fright with a Flock of Feathered Friends.

Johan Thornton

INCLUDED CONTENTS:
Five footnotes, and there's even a footnote inside a footnote.
13 curious equations or mathematical expressions, and 23 charts or signs.
A semilogarithmic linear regression plot (see Figure 3 in Appendix B).

TheFour**Frogs**.com

Proof Of Concept Publications

DISCLAIMER: While only some of the numbers used in this book are prime,
when added up together they make 100,000,000,000,000,001,417,681 which is a prime.

The Four Frogs — **An Increasingly Numerical Tale, Intensely Told**

© 2025 Johan Thornton. Most rights reserved; but you can tell this story to anyone.

Proof Of Concept Publications Group

TheFourFrogs.com

No part of this publication may be reproduced, distributed, or transmitted in any form or by any means, including photocopying, recording, quantum replication, telepathy, or other electronic or mechanical methods, without prior written permission of the publisher, except in cases of brief quotations in critical reviews, alien attacks, or certain other non-commercial uses allowed by copyright law. This is a work of friction times distance. Any perceived similarity to actual **frogs**, living or deceased, or actual events, is purely coincidental. Use only as directed. Keep within reach of children.

ISBN: 979-8-88913-228-8 (Hard cover)

This book is dedicated to my mom, who first read children's books to me (in Swedish!) and always said I could reach anything.

Pioneering Peculiar Prime Pyramid Poem Preface Puzzle*

Yo,
the
prime
numbers
are in letter
counts per line?
See as seventeen and
nineteen slowly enter,
as each new line gets longer?
Perhaps this book's sequel may have
an ever-larger sequence of the primes?
Well, that'll have to be saved for another time,
because we will now tell the tale of The Four **Frogs**
who were very Flummoxed, but Fixed a Fiendish Fright
with the huge assistance of a Flock of Feathered Friends!

---

*__Maychance__ **you w**ill be the one finding the Deliferate Mistale?†
†**Or by pure happenst**ance you find something like an Indeliferate Mistale.

PROLOGUE
A Journey through the Decimal* Positional System

one = 1

ten = 10 = 1111111111

one hundred = 100 = 10 10 10 10 10 10 10 10 10 10

one thousand = 1000 = 100 100 100 100 100 100 100 100 100 100

ten thousand = 10,000 = 1000 1000 1000 1000 1000 1000 1000 1000 1000 1000

one hundred thousand = 100,000 = 10,000 10,000 10,000 10,000 10,000 10,000 10,000 10,000 10,000 10,000

one million = 1,000,000 = 100,000 100,000 100,000 100,000 100,000 100,000 100,000 100,000 100,000 100,000

one billion = 1,000,000,000

one trillion = 1,000,000,000,000

---

*Human base-ten notation will be used in 99.9% of this story. However, if the amazing amphibians had developed mathematics before us, this book would likely have been in base eight, since frogs have four digits on each forelimb.

One day a duck told **two** little dogs
A story that started with **four** little **frogs**.

And **seven** little devils and **eleven** little elves
Who were talking all together and talking to themselves.

For the **frogs** had forgotten for the **fifteenth** time
To sweep their pond of the slimy slime!

So the **eighteen** devils and elves did say
That switching out the water was the only way.

"**Twenty-three** days," **one** devil reckons,
"And **twenty-three** hours and **twenty-three** seconds"

"Is the time for **forty-four frogs** to ferry
All the water if they carried all the water they could carry!"

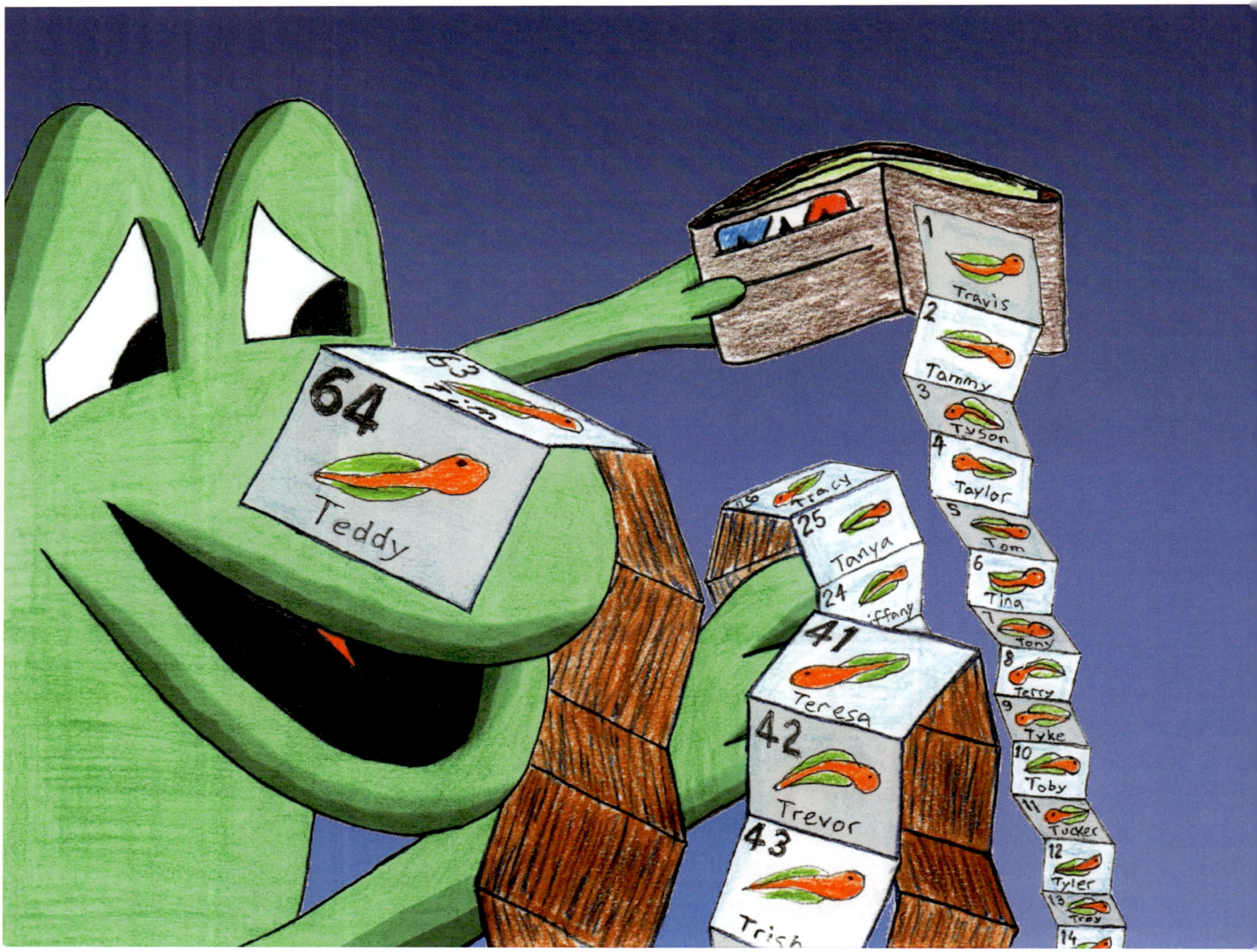

"Too long!" said a **frog**; "Too long indeed!
I've got **sixty-four** hungry **tadpoles** to feed!"

10 10 10 1 1
10 10 10 1 1

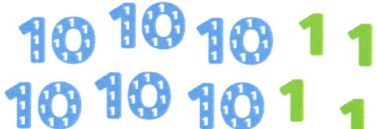

"What if instead I should happen to haul
Those **ninety-nine** bottles of bugs on the wall?"

"Enough!" said an elf, "We could scream and shout
For **a hundred** days before we figure this out!"

So the **frogs** did think — for **three hundred** blinks —
For a **frog** thinks of things the way just a **frog** thinks!

"New water!" they said, "through tricks and trials!
Through traps, through travels to **a thousand** miles!"

"We **frogs** have known for **six thousand** years
That it's never as hard as it first appears!"

1000 1000 1000
1000 1000 1000

"We'll just fill the beaks of **eight thousand** eagles,
Or sparrows, or swallows, or starlings, or seagulls!"

So the **frogs** caught a ride on the horns of a deer
To the end of a **twelve thousand** meter-long pier —

Where there were **forty-four thousand four hundred twenty**
Seagulls smiling — yes, seagulls a-plenty!

Then **forty-four thousand four twenty-four**
Smiling faces flying back from the shore!

And the sound that was heard, as down that water crashes,
Was **a hundred thousand** splishes and **a hundred thousand** splashes.

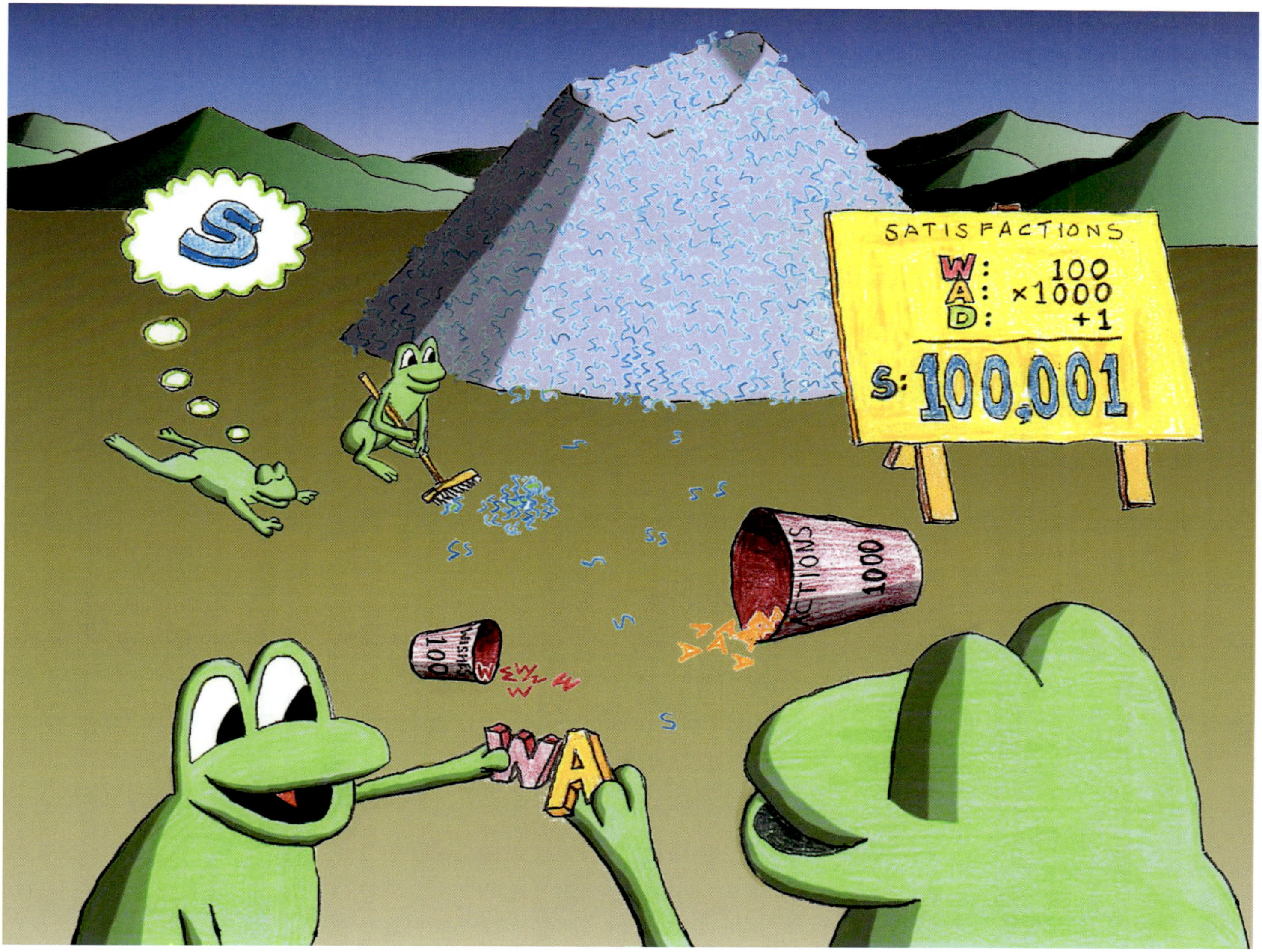

Then **a hundred** little wishes times **a thousand** little actions,
Plus **a** dream! — make **a hundred thousand one** satisfactions.

 ×  + =

Now the **frogs** all said it was **a million** times better,
And they swore this story is true to the letter.

But if you don't think it's true, I'll repeat these rhymes
One hundred thousand billion trillion times!

APPENDIX A
Word Cloud with QR Frog

Figure 1. A crowded word cloud (above) of the one hundred fifty-seven root words used in this book, sized roughly by how often they appear, except for the common words.

Figure 2. To see music videos of this book, scan the QR frog (left) or drippily visit TheFourFrogs.com.

APPENDIX B
A Semilogarithmic Numeric Distribution Plot, with References

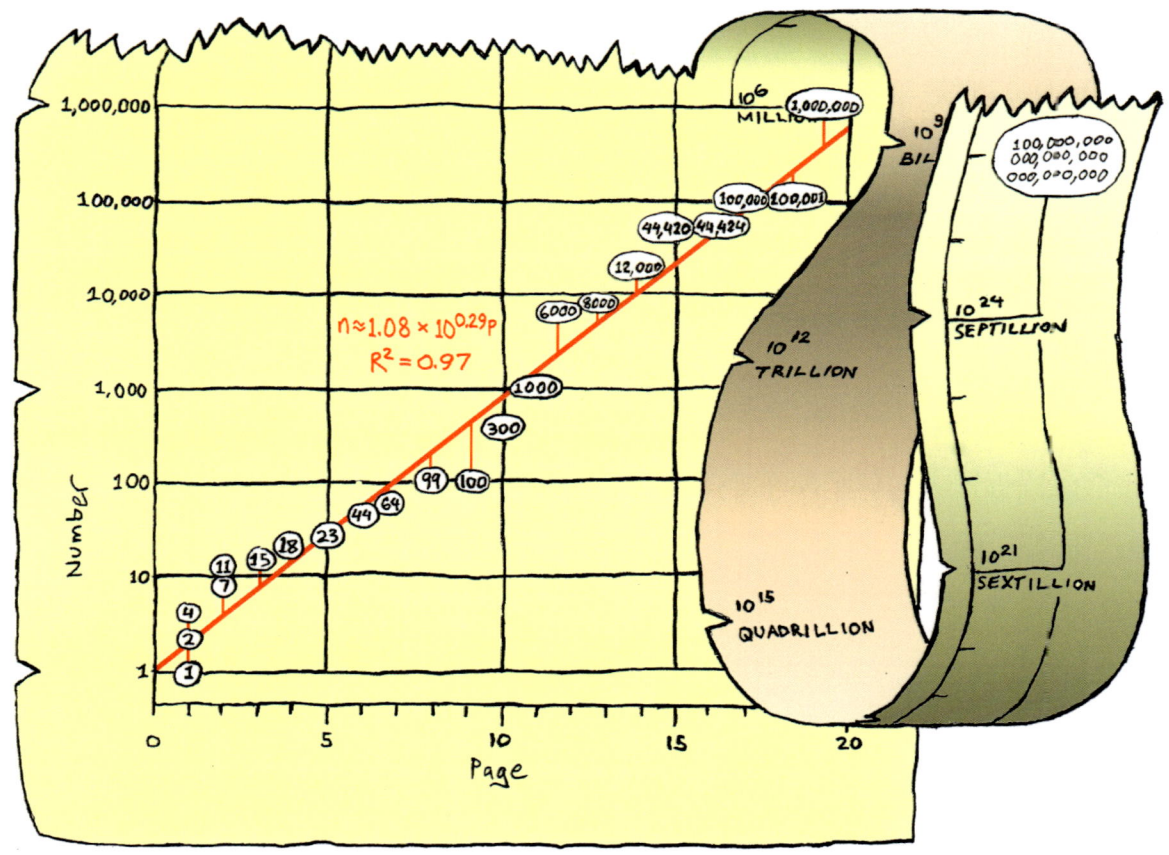

Figure 3. Frogs enjoy numbers.[1] Shown is a semilogarithmic plot of the numbers n used herein, against the page number p. A clear increasing trend can be seen,[2] confirming the subtitle (and the purpose) of this book. Linear regression shows $n \approx 1.08 \times 10^{0.29p}$ with $R^2 = 0.97$, for $1 \leq p \leq 19$, suggesting a good fit. The location and decimal power of quintillion have been left as a little challenge exercise for the reader.

---

1. **Stancher, G., Rugani, R., Regolin, L., Vallortigara, G.** "Numerical discrimination by **frogs** (Bombina orientalis)." *Animal Cognition*, vol. 18, Aug 2014, pp. 219-220.

2. **Giles, David E. A.** "Interpreting dummy variables in semi-logarithmic regression models: exact distributional results." University of Victoria, January 2011. (Econometrics Working Paper, EWP1101)

www.ingramcontent.com/pod-product-compliance
Lightning Source LLC
Chambersburg PA
CBRC091204010526
44107CB00021B/1237